AuthorHouse™
1663 Liberty Drive
Bloomington, IN 47403
www.authorhouse.com
Phone: 1 (800) 839-8640

Interior and Cover Illustrations
created by Emily Hulsey

Published by AuthorHouse 10/07/2016

ISBN: 978-1-5246-4396-6 (sc)
978-1-5246-4398-0 (hc)
978-1-5246-4397-3 (e)

Library of Congress Control Number: Pending

Print information available on the last page.

authorHOUSE®

I See...

KAT J PHILLIPS

Illustrations by Emily Hulsey

For Mama...for Love...for Life...for Forgiveness...
for Support...for Forever. You created me so I could create
beauty in the world. That beauty came from you.

Nature's Words

Nature is like a second mother to me
When I talk to her, she makes me think
About life and why people exist.
Even as I sit here in silence,
I feel I am not alone;
Nature is here to keep me safe.
Nature opens my eyes,
And I see her beauty and amazement.
When I look up at the sky,
My mind is wandering
I sort out my problems,
By looking at the truth in Nature's words.
Every time I touch a tree,
I am touching Nature's hand.
I know Nature will always be there for me.
She is the best friend I ever had.
She folds her arms around me, and I feel safe,
Like nothing will ever harm me.
And when I die,
I will be one with Nature,
Just like she always wanted me to be.

When it Snows

When it snows, everything is beautiful and glowing;
The lightness of the night seems to come from nowhere.
The deafening silence could any minute be...
Shattered by the cry of an animal.
All is peaceful and evil is scarce,
The snow moves with the wind and reminds me,
Of sand moving over the dunes.
Each snowflake has its own tale to tell,
Where it has been and what it has seen.
What I see is a world hidden within our own.

Thus was the beginning of this book. THIS is where it all began; in Junior High School. William Blake wrote, "To see the world in a grain of sand, and heaven in a wild flower." Anais Nin, "We do not see things as they are, we see things as we are." I would pick up on the nuance of a poem and the depth of its meaning. I now appreciate all of the times I was called a nerd and made fun of for being the "Teacher's Pet." Karma works in mysterious ways and now I am reaping the rewards of enduring the ridicule of my classmates. During my time alone I read everything I could, learned what I could about poetry and authors such as Poe, Whitman, Blake, Thoreau, Hemingway, and even Martin Luther.

Now, over 20 years later, I am ready to make others happy, make them think, make them weep for sadness or for joy. I want my poems and photos to be awe inspiring and make a difference in the life of another human being. Beauty is still in the world and my hope is that my books (yes, there will be others) will help Mankind find what it has been lacking and what the Human Race has been looking for; kindness, understanding, passion, grace, beauty, motivation, appreciation of each other and our world. Look up, look around, look inside!

Eternity at Sea

Our home once was
On a shore of white sand
The froth of never ending movement
Running through our hands

The moon would rise
And turn the sea to glass
Light the steps we left
Forever imprinted on our past

The cry of gulls
The call of whales
Pull me back through centuries
Remind me of our tales

Our ship in pieces
Wrecked upon the dunes
The water moves the wood
Across the land comes the eerie tune

Could we ever go back?
To the bore of the city
Tearing at our souls
Its claws without pity

Look around us now
We are free and alive
We have each other
And the need to survive

Come and sit with me
Silence is our friend
Quiet all your fears
To the waves you will bend

Free yourself
To the call of the sea
Walk into the water
The current around you be

The movement will sweep
The ebb will gather
Caressing your skin
Feel only what matters

My love for you
Dreams to forever share
Eternity in the fathoms
Your beauty will forever be there

Storm is Coming

A storm is coming
...one that will change
...everything we feel
...everything we know
...everything we want to cling too
A storm is coming
...for some
...intuition beyond belief
...a new vision of the energy
...and what the world holds.
A storm is coming
...for others
...pain neverending
...their refusal to see
...beyond their own eyes
...closed always to possibilities
A Storm is coming
...even when the lightening
...hits them head on
...so many people
...pay no attention.
A Storm is coming
...do you hear
...the rumbling of change
...the tremors of time
...the universe
...will rearrange

Grandfather Oak

Run your soft fingers,
Over his rough exterior,
Feel his powerful wisdom,
Seeping...
Out of his bark into your veins.

This gnarly old oak,
Many stories to tell,
Much history...
Teaching you,
Is your heart open to his will?

The battles...Oak has seen,
Fought by children...
Trivial quarrels,
And grown men...
Over land and machinery,
At times, causing bloody damage
For life is too fragile.

The voices this oak has listened to,
Town's people chattering
...about each other's business,
Choirs singing...
Lifting the hearts of masses,
The other gnarly old oaks,
Share in his wisdom.

This gnarly old oak,
Looks like a wise man I know,
Who sits and ponders each day,
Waiting...
Patiently...
He knows I will appear.

I walk across the front porch,
Sit in the chair beside him,
My soft skin touches his rough bark,
My blue eyes look back at me.

The gnarly oak breaks its bark,
...a smile,
He starts to tell me about his life,
What he remembers of mine,
I will always treasure,
The love...
The memories...
...of My Grandfather Oak

The Delicate Flower

Delicate flower,
> Hold your head high,
>> Remember what I taught you,
>>> Do not let life pass you by.

Delicate flower,
> Raise your arms to the sun
>> Remember what I said,
>>> And to you, will come no harm.

Delicate flower,
> Keep your feet free and light,
>> Remember what I said,
>>> A fire inside you, the spirits did ignite.

Delicate flower
> Stand your ground,
>> Remember what I said,
>>> Your soul will be free and unbound.

Delicate flower
> Keep me in your heart,
>> Remember the promise I said,
>>> We will never be apart.

© 2011 Kat J Phillips

Dedicated to my niece Ashley-Kate Hale.
The name Ashley, is a family name from our Great
Grandfathers. Kate…well…
Love you forever Power Flower! - Auntie Kate

My Dream

Once in a while there comes a time,
When I decide your world can be mine,
I open my soul,
My heart drifting on the wind,
My mind like the ocean,
Vast and ever deep.
I draw on my power,
Now hear my chime.

Come to me now,
I can show you the way,
We can live together,
Eat, sleep, work, and play.
Wake to greet the morning,
Of each passing day,
She is calling to thee,
I will keep you safe,
So never go astray.

On stone, stable ground,
A place for us to share,
Every room filled with lavender,
And the smell of your hair.
Try as I might,
Look away to the sun,
But at you I always stare,
I do these things out of love,
Because for you…
I care.

Remember with me,
You will always belong,
In our hidden forest,
The days of your longing,
Are forever done..................

Wait...
I feel something creeping,
Like oil from the ground,
Coming, it is seeping,
Look here is the dawn,
I was only dreaming,
You are really gone.

Rain Down

Sliding down the blades of grass
We ebb and flow to the soft earth
Disappear within
Sinking down to the depths below

Soft and gentle we caress the trees
The buildings and the people
We are there to wash away the sorrow
When a loved one is laid to rest

Other times we come in a torrent
And do not disappear into the dirt
We rush across the land
Sweeping
Away the debris and the leaves
The rocks and the stones
The loose rumble not held down
All is necessary
Without us
The world could not survive

Rain down is what we do
Falling from the sky above
Rolling down the hills
Sliding across the rooftops
Drops onto the heads of tiny children
Who find us fun and fill with laughter

Our most favorite feeling
Is a child's foot
With force of will and strength of abandon
Splashed into our puddles
Caring not what is soaked by Our Rain

Dawn

Dawn
Many think of time
Space of beauty
Sit and watch her rise
A moment of quiet
Solace in a world
…of chaos and wrath

Color painting
Across the land bathing
My face
A splash of warmth
Waking the ancestral being
Laying deep within

Dawn
The idea of you
Brings me to my knees
To behold your grace again
…be blessed by your touch
Tingling on my body
Once more

The birds
Praise your existence
Animals wake
Be scarce
When…
… your beauty appears

The woodlands stir
 Creatures skittering
    …the Owl
      She retires
…buries Her head
Under a wing
      Safe inside the tree
The shadow cast by your light

Dawn
 It has been many moons
Since last I sat with thee
…forgotten nothing
      All the secrets
      Told to me
 In the whisper of the wind

The change in my life
    …now I
      …wait for you
That first light
Bring us to safety
      The Owl
      She sleeps
Protected by the shadow
      Of Dawn

I Need

I need to hear your voice every morning
To wake the sun to brighten my day
To start the birds singing
To start the cathedral chimes

I need to see into your eyes
Peering at the world and know
Seeing the best inside
Looking into my soul.

I need to feel your touch
The current running from your fingers
Then holds me close while I am weeping
Glinting stars, my tears fall

I need to hear you say my name
To chase the pain and wake the sun
To start the sound of morning rain
Remind I have so much to gain

I need you to see into my eyes
The sadness you chased away
The knowledge deep in my heart
I'll live to see another day

I need to feel these things
To know with happiness I am blessed
I need you to know
Your courage
Helps my Stars to rest

Druids Judgment

Up the hill
Treading the familiar path
Toward the pillar I stand upon
...to judge

The walk
...for joy
...for heartache
...for right or for wrong
My duty is set
Cannot turn my back
...on destiny
...she has gifted me

On the pillar
I now stand
...to offer praise
For those who honor our tribe
Bring forth courage
...gifts of delight
...a new height of rank
...pride for their family

For those who disgrace
...those who streak of yellow
My judgment
...is swift and harsh
As is the others
...who stand beside me
Pillars filled with wisdom

The five working in tandem
Deciding
...the fate of the one being judged
...hard labor
...endless torture
Or the most merciful
...deaths swift blade
...to avoid the shame

I was chosen
By the powers of great height
For my heart is a balance
...see past my personal feelings
...pushed aside
See only the deeds done
...deeds are what remain
...the judgment to be handed
Balanced

Wind Blows...Fire Burns

Wind blows,
...the fire burns.
The passion inside her,
...to right what is wrong.
Wind blows,
...the fire burns.
The horrid eating at her soul,
...to rid the world of hate.

Wind blows,
...the fire burns.
Do no try to be unyielding
...alternatives are none.
Wind blows,
...the fire burns.
The one with no boundaries,
...no limiting,
...fearless.

Wind blows,
...the fire burns.
Your coals of bitterness,
...fuel for her iron hammer,
...the sense,
You should have seen coming,
...now impales your door.

Wind blows,

...the fire burns.

Even as her body is battered,

...marks left by the scars of mystic battle,

...matters not to her.

What is wronged,

...must be revenged,

...what is weak,

...must be put to mend.

Wind blows,

...the fire burns.

To cross her is folly,

...to follow is wisdom.

Only if you wield your own fire,

...her wind fuels the flare.

Wind blows,

...the fire burns.

Will you walk the path,

...it existed for centuries.

Are you just now seeing...

She is the wind that blows,

She is the fire that burns.

...the one who decides,

...worthy,

...not.

<u>Background</u>: *In Shawnee, KS at Shawnee Mission Medical Center there is a small outdoor sitting area that I used to sit in and eat dinner when I was a junior volunteer. When I was a patient with a new pacemaker in my chest, my room was right above this area. The tree that was once the same height as me, had grown so tall it now reached over the roof. I felt this tree was an old friend and I was meant to be in that room. I felt the tree was telling me; you will grow and live on, just as I have. So, the poem was created by inspiration of a tree I have known for more than 20 years. ©2014 Kat J Phillips*

<u>The Tree</u>

The tree
Just put in
Soaking up her surroundings
...feeling small.
Not certain if she will thrive
...uncertain of any growth at all.

The tree
Now settled
...her roots spreading out.
Feel for the warmth
...finding the nourishment
...standing a little taller
Reaching out for more light.

The tree
Now a pillar in the dark woods
Making herself known
...other trees seek her shade
...animals hide inside her trunk.
She feels comfort
...no longer alone.

The Tree
Now on firm soil
Her place she has found
...roots have taken hold
...no longer fears the wind.
They may blow against her will
Strong
...she stands unwavering.

The Tree
Her branches growing taller
Her leaves a brighter emerald
...fear of losing her hold.
...blows away with the wind
Now she stands free.

The Tree
Dancing in the woods.
The others around watching
...finding hope in the dance.
That one day freedom will be had
...by others on her same path.

The Tree
...firmly planted
Must now let go of her seedlings
...start the journey on.
To another wood
...with the wind
...fly on the seeds.
To the next new surroundings
...once again try to take hold.

Sorrow or Tranquility

I have a secret
...one I want to share.
This secret is sacred
...mine alone too bare.
I've been to the ether
...to the bright
...the white
...the peace.
I've seen what is waiting
...when my heart truly does cease.

If only
...you knew
...what lies beyond.
All you've heard is true
Death is...
...a Dawn.
A beginning
...not an end.

A pathway of your life
...visions of what you've wrought
Did you cause happiness
...or force another into strife?

That is the part that's secret
...now I'm the one that knows.
When I meet someone
...what path they have bestowed.
So hard to look at humanity
...to see into their eyes.
If what waits for them is sorrow
...on the other side.

At times...
...there is peace
...tranquility like the sea.
Warmth builds inside me
...for this person
...blessed be.

So here again
..:yet another gift
...upon me has been bestowed.
Unique this one is
...never able to stop the flow.
All humanity
...if I look into their eyes
...capture what I see.
I know what waits for you
...after death
...sorrow or tranquility.

Alive

I've walked through life
Been down many roads
I have never found you
...only burdening loads

Lost on my way
Never to find
...just one peaceful day
The forest is thick
...drowning me in
Trouble finding strength
...there is none within

That light up ahead
It cannot be
Always lost in the dark
...am unable to see
Find my way
...by stumbling
Crawling on my hands and knees
Never reaching a destination
...nothing accomplished
...nothing worth the journey

There it is again
...light
...you haunt me
Toying and playing
...in my sight
I hide away from the teasing
...what cannot be

Crawl under the dirt and leaves
...never see day again
Cold and dark
Lost under this blanket
...familiar keeping me warm
Alive

Wasteland

Our feet make no sound
Walking across the piles of bones
The skulls that scattered
We use as stepping stones

So many have fallen
A resolution we have yet to see
Why we could do nothing sooner
About what was meant to be

The field of battle
Lies just beyond the hills
We are ready to defend
Even if it kills

Growing our bond
Drawing on inner strength
We move toward the rust
Driven forward by instinct

Our blessing will come
When all the flames expire
The road between the hills
Looks oh so forever dire

I remember what was said
Our souls will go on
Clawed by the undead
Who will never see the dawn

With our bond guiding our feet
We tread across the rocky terrain
Miles forever, the journey we are taking
On our bodies begins the strain

The spirit of each other
Is what we draw from
Our hearts remain strong
Beating as one

Our knowledge and future vision
Compel us to carry on
Unsure of what lies ahead
Forward we march
Through the land of the dead

Through the darkness
The stench and the tears
We continue the path forward
Ready with our spears

Only we can see
The light that guides our way
It is our greatest strength
Against the emptiness that preys

Our bond is watching and guiding
The faith in our abilities burns
We stand unyielding
Our faces stern

Enemies hide, snipe and deceive
They will soon know the lesson
They are meant to receive

Through the pass now
And on around the bend
The Ones chosen for battle
Are beginning the end.

Silence

Silence…
There never is!
Always a screaming,
A crying child,
The yelling of a man,
Echoes across my land,
Of the harbor in my mind.
Silence…
Does not exist!
Inside…
Chaos reigns.
Running away,
Foot falls on hard land.
Hiding under a bed,
Being drug down a hall,
Thrown down the stairs,
Crashing on the head,
Of the harbor in my mind.
Silence…
I am never allowed!
More memories every day,
Rise to the surface,
Break the water tension.
Climb their way out,
Of boxes I thought I had locked away,
Unraveling the ropes and knots,
Of the harbor in my mind.

Silence
I have forgotten you old friend!
To not hear the crying,
To not hear the screaming,
To not hear the laughter of evil,
Echo across the land.
All the time,
The nails driven deeper,
Into my soulless stretch of expanse.
Of the harbor in my mind.

Silence
I will miss you!
I know I will never again,
Have you?
The voices in my head are winning,
Running across the land,
Chasing each other for control,
Running each other down,
I know there will never be,
A place of quiet,
In the harbor in my mind.
Silence

©2014 Kat J Phillips

Flowers of Evil – Part II

Flowers of Evil
  Thought I could rid
  The seeds that have slid
  But still they remain
  Growing and change

Flowers of Evil
  Evolved into
  Changed into
  What you needed to be
  In order to remain
With in me

Flowers of Evil
  Crafty and spry
  Hidden away
  Buried deep,
Patient
  Waiting for your day

Flowers of Evil
  Have sprung forth again
  To torment me
  Speak to me
Taunt me
  To reach within

Flowers of Evil
  As I feel you grow
  I feel myself give in
  The Grin of Evil appears again

Flowers of Evil
Will I ever be rid
Will you be just like the darkness
Just like the chaos
Just like the lack of Silence

Flowers of Evil
I cannot decide
If I will miss you
If I will follow you
As I follow darkness
As I follow chaos
As I listen to Silence

Flowers of Evil
Do not leave me
For without you
Not able to see you
I could never be

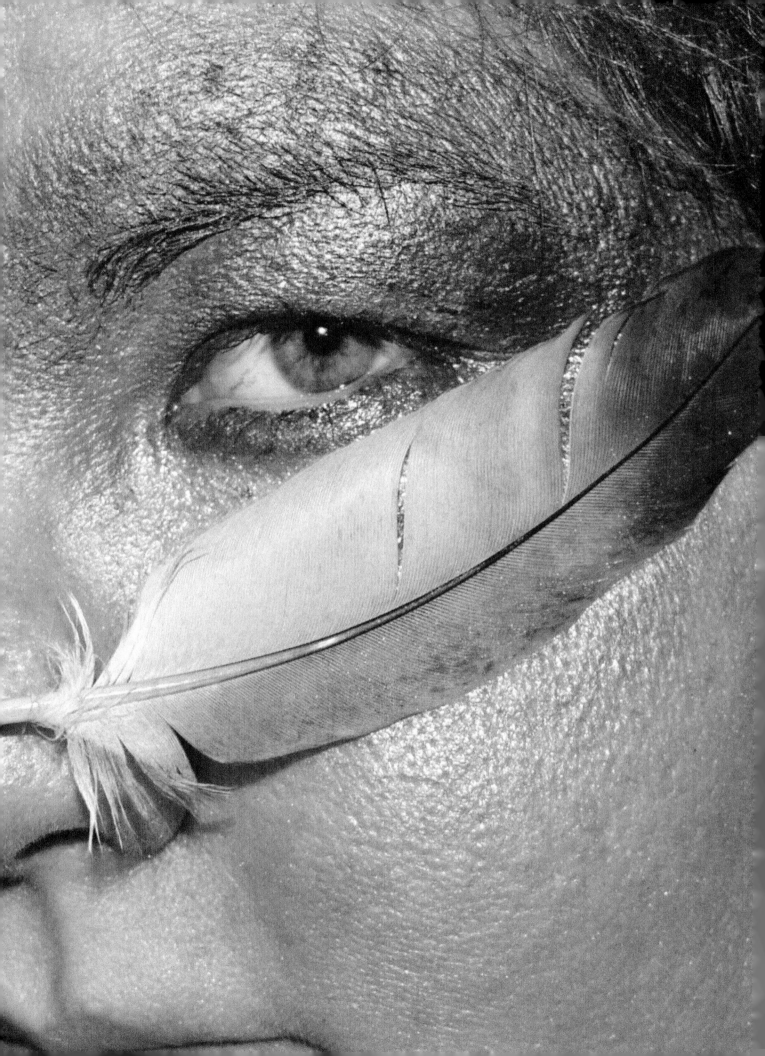

I See

I see
> What others refuse to see

I am
> What others refuse to be

I live
> What others choose to ignore

I can
> When others refuse the chore

I will
> What others turn their backs on

I try
> What others fear to bank on

I walk
> Where others fear to tread

I stand
> When others hide their head

I free
> What others try too hinder

I look
> When others refuse the splendor

I see
> What others refuse to see

I see
> Because I choose to be

Do You?

CPSIA information can be obtained
at www.ICGtesting.com
Printed in the USA
LVOW05*2055050517
533436LV00006B/6/P

9 781524 643980